# Navigating the Depths

## Unraveling the Complex Tapestry of Humanistic Psychology

**Freudian Trips**

# Copyright Page

# Disclaimer

The views and opinions expressed in this book are those of the author(s) and do not necessarily reflect the official policy or position of any other agency, organization, employer, or company. The contents of this book are for informational and educational purposes only and are not intended to serve as professional advice, diagnosis, or treatment.

The information provided in this book is believed to be accurate and reliable as of the date of publication. However, it may include some errors or inaccuracies, and no warranty or guarantee is provided regarding the accuracy, timeliness, or applicability of the content.

Readers are encouraged to consult with professional philosophers, educators, or other qualified professionals where appropriate for personalized advice. The author(s) and publisher shall not be liable for any loss, damage, or harm caused or alleged to be caused, directly or indirectly, by the information or ideas contained, suggested, or referenced in this book.

By reading this book, the reader acknowledges and agrees that they are solely responsible for how they interpret and apply the information contained herein.

This book may also include references to other works, studies, and sources. These references are provided for further reading and exploration and do not imply endorsement or validation of the specific theories, viewpoints, or interpretations presented in those works.

# Chapter 1: Introduction

Welcome to the fascinating world of humanistic psychology, a field that celebrates the unique and multifaceted nature of human beings. A psychological viewpoint known as "humanistic psychology" places a strong emphasis on the value of each individual's inherent worth, self-actualization, and personal development. It is an approach that sees people as more than just the sum of their parts, recognizing the complexity and depth of human experience.

**A Brief Overview of Humanistic Psychology:**

At the core of humanistic psychology is the belief that each person has the potential to grow, learn, and develop into the best version of themselves. This growth is facilitated by embracing our innermost feelings, thoughts, and experiences, allowing us to live more authentic and fulfilling lives. The goal of humanistic psychology is to help individuals realize their full potential and live a life that is true to themselves.

**Historical Context and Emergence:**

The roots of humanistic psychology can be traced back to the early 20th century when psychologists began to challenge the dominant paradigms of the time, such as behaviorism and psychoanalysis. These traditional approaches often viewed humans as passive recipients of external forces or as being driven by unconscious desires and conflicts.

In contrast, humanistic psychology emerged as a "third force" that emphasized the active role of individuals in shaping their own lives. It was a response to the dehumanizing aspects of the industrial revolution and the devastation of two world wars, which left many people questioning the nature of humanity.

Some of the key figures in the development of humanistic psychology include Abraham Maslow, Carl Rogers, and Rollo May. These pioneers laid the groundwork for a new way of understanding human behavior and experience, one that recognized the importance of personal growth, self-actualization, and the intrinsic value of each person.

In summary, humanistic psychology is a rich and vibrant field that offers a refreshing and empowering perspective on human nature. It is an approach that celebrates the uniqueness and potential of each individual, recognizing that we all have the ability to grow, learn, and develop into the best version of ourselves. As we delve deeper into this fascinating world, we will explore the key concepts, major figures, and practical applications of humanistic psychology, gaining a deeper understanding of what it means to be human.

# Chapter 2: Key Concepts in Humanistic Psychology

Humanistic psychology is built on a foundation of core principles that highlight the importance of personal growth, self-actualization, and healthy relationships. Let's explore some of these key concepts to better understand what makes humanistic psychology so unique and valuable.

**Self-Actualization:**

Self-actualization is like reaching the pinnacle of your own personal mountain. It's about realizing your full potential and becoming the best version of yourself. Imagine a flower reaching towards the sunlight, growing and blooming into its most beautiful form. That's what self-actualization is all about. It's the process of discovering who you truly are, embracing your strengths and weaknesses, and living a life that is true to yourself.

**Personal Growth**:

Personal growth is closely linked to self-actualization. It's about accepting new experiences, growing from setbacks, and always changing as a person. Just like a tree adds new rings as it grows, we too can add new layers to our character and personality as we navigate through life's journey.

## Congruence:

Congruence is a fancy word that simply means being genuine and true to yourself. It's about aligning your actions with your values and beliefs, and being the same person on the inside as you are on the outside. Imagine wearing a mask that hides your true self; congruence is about taking off that mask and showing the world who you really are.

## Unconditional Positive Regard:

Unconditional positive regard is a term coined by Carl Rogers, one of the pioneers of humanistic psychology. It refers to the idea of accepting and valuing others for who they are, without judgment or conditions. It's like a parent's love for their child; no matter what the child does, the parent still loves and accepts them unconditionally.

## Empathy:

Empathy is the ability to understand and share the feelings of another person. It's about putting yourself in someone else's shoes and seeing the world from their perspective. Imagine walking a mile in someone else's shoes; empathy is about truly understanding and feeling what that person is going through.

In summary, these key concepts of humanistic psychology provide a framework for understanding the importance of personal growth, self-actualization, and healthy relationships. By embracing these principles, we can live more authentic and fulfilling lives, building deeper connections with ourselves and those around us.

# Chapter 3: Major Figures in Humanistic Psychology

Just as every story has its heroes, humanistic psychology has been shaped and molded by a cast of remarkable individuals who have made significant contributions to the field. Let's meet some of these major figures and explore the unique ideas they brought to the world of psychology.

**Abraham Maslow:**

Abraham Maslow is best known for his concept of the "hierarchy of needs," which is often depicted as a pyramid. At the base of the pyramid are our basic needs, like food and shelter, while at the top is self-actualization, the ultimate goal of personal growth and fulfillment. Maslow believed that once our basic needs are met, we can then focus on achieving our full potential as human beings.

**Carl Rogers:**

Carl Rogers introduced the idea of "client-centered therapy," a groundbreaking approach that emphasizes the importance of the individual in the therapeutic process. He believed that given the right conditions, people have the innate ability to heal themselves. Rogers also introduced the concept of "unconditional positive regard," which we discussed in the previous chapter.

## Rollo May:

Rollo May brought a philosophical touch to humanistic psychology, drawing on the works of existential philosophers like Søren Kierkegaard and Jean-Paul Sartre. He believed that anxiety and inner conflict arise from the challenges of human existence, such as the struggle for freedom and the search for meaning. May's work highlighted the importance of facing these challenges head-on in order to live a more authentic and fulfilling life.

## Charlotte Bühler:

Charlotte Bühler was one of the first psychologists to focus on the study of human development across the lifespan. She believed that personal growth and self-actualization are lifelong processes, and that people continue to evolve and grow throughout their lives. Bühler's work paved the way for future research in the field of developmental psychology.

## Viktor Frankl:

Viktor Frankl survived the horrors of the Holocaust and used his experiences to develop a new approach to psychology known as "logotherapy." Frankl held that humans may discover meaning and purpose in life, even in the most trying situations, and that this desire for meaning is what propels human existence. His book, "Man's Search for Meaning," is considered one of the most influential works in the field of psychology.

In summary, these major figures in humanistic psychology have each contributed unique and valuable ideas that have shaped the field as we know it today. Their work continues to inspire and guide those who seek to understand the complexities of human nature and the importance of personal growth and self-actualization.

# Chapter 4: Humanistic Psychology in Practice

Humanistic psychology isn't just a theory confined to textbooks; it has practical applications that touch many aspects of our lives. From therapy rooms to classrooms, boardrooms to hospital rooms, the principles of humanistic psychology are used to foster personal growth, improve relationships, and enhance well-being. Let's take a closer look at some of these applications.

**Psychotherapy:**

One of the primary areas where humanistic psychology has had a significant impact is in psychotherapy. Humanistic therapists focus on creating a supportive and accepting environment that encourages clients to explore their thoughts and feelings without fear of judgment. This approach helps individuals gain insight into their behavior and fosters personal growth and self-acceptance.

**Education:**

Humanistic principles have also been applied to the field of education, where they have been used to create more student-centered learning environments. In these settings, teachers act as facilitators rather than authoritarian figures, helping students develop their own interests and abilities. This approach recognizes the importance of personal growth and self-discovery in the learning process.

## Organizational Development:

In the business world, humanistic psychology has been used to improve organizational development and leadership. Humanistic principles are employed to create more supportive and collaborative work environments, where employees are valued for their unique contributions. This strategy encourages invention, creativity, and a feeling of community, which eventually boosts output and increases job satisfaction.

## Health and Well-being:

Finally, humanistic psychology has been applied to the field of health and well-being. This approach recognizes the importance of emotional and psychological factors in physical health and utilizes techniques such as mindfulness and positive psychology to enhance overall well-being. By focusing on the whole person, humanistic psychology helps individuals build resilience, find meaning in their experiences, and live more fulfilling lives.

In summary, the principles of humanistic psychology are not just theoretical concepts; they have practical applications that touch many aspects of our lives. From therapy rooms to classrooms, boardrooms to hospital rooms, humanistic psychology is used to foster personal growth, improve relationships, and enhance overall well-being. By embracing the principles of humanistic psychology, we can live more authentic and fulfilling lives, building deeper connections with ourselves and those around us.

# Chapter 5: Critiques and Limitations of Humanistic Psychology

While humanistic psychology has made significant contributions to our understanding of human nature and personal growth, it is not without its critiques and limitations. It is important to consider these criticisms to have a well-rounded understanding of the field. Let's explore some of the main critiques of humanistic psychology.

**Lack of Empirical Support:**

One of the main criticisms of humanistic psychology is that it lacks empirical support. In other words, some of the concepts and theories in humanistic psychology are difficult to test and measure scientifically. For example, how do you measure self-actualization or congruence? This lack of empirical support has led some critics to question the validity and reliability of humanistic psychology as a scientific discipline.

**Cultural Bias:**

Another criticism of humanistic psychology is that it may have a cultural bias. Many of the theories and concepts in humanistic psychology were developed by Western psychologists and may not be applicable to people from other cultural backgrounds. This cultural bias can limit the universality and applicability of humanistic psychology, as it may not fully take into account the diverse range of human experiences and values.

**Overemphasis on Positivity:**

Finally, some critics argue that humanistic psychology places too much emphasis on positivity and personal growth, potentially overlooking the darker or more challenging aspects of human nature. For example, humanistic psychology may not fully address issues such as aggression, mental illness, or social inequality. This overemphasis on positivity can create an idealized and unrealistic view of human nature, neglecting the complexities and challenges that are an inherent part of the human experience.

In summary, while humanistic psychology has made valuable contributions to our understanding of human nature and personal growth, it is not without its critiques and limitations. The lack of empirical support, cultural bias, and overemphasis on positivity are all valid criticisms that need to be addressed in order to have a more complete and balanced view of humanistic psychology. It is important to recognize these limitations while also appreciating the unique insights and perspectives that humanistic psychology brings to the field.

# Chapter 6: Integrative Approaches and Contemporary Developments

As the field of psychology has evolved, so too has humanistic psychology. Researchers and practitioners have sought to integrate humanistic principles with other psychological theories, incorporate findings from neuroscience, and embrace multicultural perspectives. Let's take a closer look at some of these contemporary developments.

**Integration with Other Psychological Theories:**

Humanistic psychology has not existed in isolation. Over time, there has been a growing recognition of the value of integrating humanistic principles with other psychological theories, such as cognitive-behavioral therapy and psychoanalysis. This integrative approach allows for a more comprehensive understanding of human behavior, taking into account the complexities and nuances of the human experience.

**Neuroscientific Research:**

In recent years, there has been an increasing interest in exploring the neurological basis of humanistic concepts, such as self-actualization and empathy. Neuroscientific research has provided valuable insights into the brain processes underlying these concepts, helping to bridge the gap between the psychological and biological aspects of human behavior. This research has also helped to validate some of the principles of humanistic psychology, providing empirical support for its theories.

## Multicultural Perspectives:

Another important development in humanistic psychology has been the incorporation of multicultural perspectives. Recognizing the importance of cultural context in shaping human behavior, humanistic psychologists have sought to incorporate the values, beliefs, and experiences of diverse cultural groups. This multicultural approach helps to ensure that humanistic psychology is relevant and applicable to a wide range of individuals, regardless of their cultural background.

In summary, humanistic psychology has evolved over time, embracing new ideas and perspectives. The integration of humanistic principles with other psychological theories, the incorporation of neuroscientific research, and the inclusion of multicultural perspectives have all contributed to the growth and development of the field. These contemporary developments help to ensure that humanistic psychology remains a relevant and valuable approach to understanding the complexities of human behavior.

# Chapter 7: Applications of Humanistic Psychology

Humanistic psychology is not just a theoretical framework; it has practical applications that can have a profound impact on individuals and society. Let's take a closer look at some hypothetical case studies and practical examples to illustrate the positive impact of humanistic psychology.

**Hypothetical Case Studies and Practical Examples:**

**Hypothetical Case Study 1:** Jane's Journey to Self-Actualization

Jane, a 30-year-old woman, felt stuck in a job she didn't enjoy and struggled with low self-esteem. Through humanistic therapy, she was able to explore her thoughts and feelings in a supportive and non-judgmental environment. This process helped Jane gain insight into her values and aspirations, leading her to make changes in her career and personal life. Today, Jane feels more confident and fulfilled, having taken steps towards self-actualization.

**Hypothetical Case Study 2: Building Empathy in the Classroom:**

Mr. Smith, a high school teacher, decided to incorporate humanistic principles into his teaching methods. He focused on creating a supportive and empathetic classroom environment, where students felt valued and respected. This approach fostered a positive learning atmosphere, where students were more engaged and motivated to learn. Mr. Smith observed improvements in students' academic performance and overall well-being.

**Positive Impact on Individuals and Society:**

The principles of humanistic psychology have the potential to bring about positive change in individuals and society as a whole. By emphasizing the importance of personal growth, self-actualization, and healthy relationships, humanistic psychology empowers individuals to live more authentic and fulfilling lives. This can therefore result in a society that is more peaceful and compassionate, where individuals are more understanding and helpful to one another.

In summary, the applications of humanistic psychology are diverse and far-reaching, with the potential to positively impact individuals and society. Hypothetical case studies and practical examples illustrate the transformative power of humanistic principles, highlighting the importance of personal growth, empathy, and positive relationships. By embracing the values of humanistic psychology, we can create a more compassionate and harmonious society, where individuals are empowered to reach their full potential.

# Chapter 8: Future Directions in Humanistic Psychology

As we look to the future, humanistic psychology continues to evolve and adapt to the changing world. New trends and research areas are emerging, there is potential for collaboration and interdisciplinary work, and ethical considerations and challenges must be addressed. Let's explore these future directions in more detail.

**Emerging Trends and Research Areas:**

Humanistic psychology is expanding its reach, exploring new and exciting areas of research. Some of these emerging trends include the integration of technology in therapy, such as online counseling and virtual reality therapy. Additionally, researchers are investigating the role of humanistic principles in addressing global issues, such as climate change and social injustice.

**Potential for Collaboration and Interdisciplinary Work:**

There is a growing recognition of the potential for collaboration between humanistic psychology and other disciplines, such as neuroscience, sociology, and philosophy. Interdisciplinary work can provide a more comprehensive understanding of human behavior, taking into account the biological, social, and philosophical aspects of the human experience. This collaborative approach can lead to new insights and innovative solutions to complex problems.

## Ethical Considerations and Challenges:

As humanistic psychology continues to evolve, ethical considerations and challenges must be addressed. For example, the use of technology in therapy raises questions about privacy and confidentiality. Additionally, humanistic psychologists must be mindful of cultural sensitivity and the potential for bias in their work. Navigating these ethical considerations and challenges is essential to maintaining the integrity and effectiveness of humanistic psychology.

In summary, the future of humanistic psychology is bright, with exciting new trends and research areas emerging. The potential for collaboration and interdisciplinary work can lead to new insights and innovative solutions to complex problems. However, ethical considerations and challenges must be addressed to ensure the integrity and effectiveness of humanistic psychology. By embracing these future directions, humanistic psychology will continue to be a valuable and relevant approach to understanding the complexities of human behavior.

# Chapter 9: Conclusion

As we reach the conclusion of our exploration into humanistic psychology, let's take a moment to recapitulate the key points we've discussed and reflect on the significance of this approach in understanding human nature.

**Recapitulation of Key Points:**

**Humanistic psychology emphasizes the importance of personal growth, self-actualization, and the intrinsic value of each person.**

**Key concepts include self-actualization, personal growth, congruence, unconditional positive regard, and empathy.**

**Major figures such as Abraham Maslow, Carl Rogers, Rollo May, Charlotte Bühler, and Viktor Frankl have contributed significantly to the field.**

**Humanistic psychology has practical applications in psychotherapy, education, organizational development, and health and well-being.**

**Despite its contributions, humanistic psychology has faced critiques such as a lack of empirical support, cultural bias, and overemphasis on positivity.**

**The field continues to evolve, embracing new trends, interdisciplinary work, and addressing ethical challenges.**

**The Significance of Humanistic Psychology in Understanding Human Nature:**

Humanistic psychology has had a profound impact on our understanding of human nature. This method offers a novel and powerful viewpoint on what it is to be human by emphasizing the distinctive and positive features of the human experience. Humanistic psychology places a strong emphasis on self-actualization and personal development in order to support people in leading more genuine and satisfying lives. Humanistic psychology's tenets can also promote a more sympathetic and peaceful community in which members are more understanding and helpful to one another.

In summary, humanistic psychology offers a valuable and unique perspective on human nature. Its emphasis on personal growth, self-actualization, and healthy relationships is relevant and applicable to various aspects of our lives. The field continues to evolve, embracing new ideas and perspectives, and addressing ethical challenges. By appreciating the contributions and significance of humanistic psychology, we can better understand ourselves and the world around us, ultimately leading to a more compassionate and harmonious society.

# About Freudian Trips

Welcome to Freudian Trips, your dedicated platform for diving deep into the world of psychology. We are more than just a YouTube channel or a book publisher. We are a beacon of enlightenment, making complex psychological concepts accessible and engaging for all.

Our YouTube channel is a rich repository of psychology made simple. We take the profound and often complex ideas from the world of psychology and break them down into digestible, easy-to-understand content. From the foundational theories of Freud to the cognitive insights of Piaget, we cover a broad spectrum of psychological schools and thoughts, making psychology accessible to everyone, regardless of their background or prior knowledge.

As a book publisher, we take the same approach, transforming intricate psychological theories into comprehensible narratives. Our books are not just collections of words, but vessels of wisdom that make psychology approachable and relatable. We believe that psychology should not be confined to academic circles, but should be available to all who seek to understand the human mind and behavior.

At Freudian Trips, we believe in the power of curiosity and the pursuit of knowledge. We are here to stoke the fires of your curiosity, to guide you on your intellectual journey, and to help you navigate the fascinating world of psychology.

If you are someone who is not afraid to question, to explore, and to learn, then you are in the right place. Join us on this journey of exploration, as we make psychology easy to understand, one concept at a time.

Be sure to visit our Youtube channel at: www.freudiantrips.com/youtube

You can also visit us on the web at www.freudiantrips.com

Welcome to The Freudian Trip community. Stay curious. Stay enlightened.